The Spiritual Philosophy of...
The Prodigal Soul

M. L. Stolte

Copyright © 2002 by M. L. Stolte First Edition
All rights reserved. This book may not be duplicated in any way without the express written consent of the publisher, except in the form of brief excerpts or quotations for the purposes of review.

Published by:
SunStone Ventures, Inc.
PO Box 39064
Sarasota, Florida 34238

www.prodigalsoul.com

Printed in the United States of America

Cover Concept: SunStone Ventures, Inc.
Cover Design: indypub, LLC

Cataloging-in-Publication Data
(Prepared by Quality Books, Inc.)

Stolte, M. L.
    The spiritual philosophy of the prodigal soul / M.L. Stolte.- - 1st ed.
    p. cm.
    LCCN 2002101826
    ISBN 0-9718033-0-7

    1. Soul. 2. Spiritualism (Philosophy) 3. Spiritual life. I. Title.

BD423.S76 2002   128.1
                            QBI02-701231

Acknowledgements

This first edition of *The Spiritual Philosophy of The Prodigal Soul* was made possible by a small number of people who helped to bring it into being through an unwavering belief in the importance and significance of the content.

Foremost is Meredith G. Reiff, who not only acted as the catalyst for the documenting of these philosophies, but who also made it possible to accomplish by providing both the environment and means to do so, every step of the way.

Much gratitude to Dr. Sid Weathermon, friend and retired English teacher who provided editing throughout the course of this project—all from the goodness of his heart. Comprehensive final editing was graciously provided by longtime friend, Christiane Francin, regardless of a schedule precluding yet more work.

Many thanks to Janice Phelps and Sonja Beal for generously sharing guidance and professional expertise. Also, to Micky Taylor, Rick Brothers, and Dotty Stolte, all who offered support and shared input on this project.

Finally, thank you Mom, Margaret Sheeder, for your help, love and enduring sweetness.

Introduction

Have you ever felt that there is more to you than meets the eye—that something within you is *deeper?* Do you ever wonder how you seem to know things you have not been taught? Do you ever feel an association — a kinship — with someone you have just met and wonder why? Do you feel that you have little in common with people of other religions? Many of us have forgotten our primary nature as God's children. The world has made it all too easy for us to forget that spiritual truth is the same for people of every religion and faith. *The Spiritual Philosophy of The Prodigal Soul* is the product of a long search to make spiritual sense out of a chaotic, seemingly unspiritual world. The good news is that the search has a great ending because we are more—a great deal more.

Opinions and views on religion, spirituality, and immortality are not hard to find, but for me, there was always something missing. Not all of the pieces of the spiritual puzzle seemed to fit. Reincarnation, with or without religious doctrine, did not answer all of my questions. Deeper exploration revealed yet more mysteries. The basic concept of reincarnation did make sense on an eternal level and potentially answered many ethereal questions. The idea of souls returning to earth seemed to bridge the gap between religious doctrine and spirituality revealed through experience. It became clear that there is a difference between organized religion and spirituality itself.

Over a ten-year period, Jesus visited me in dreams three times. These were remarkably different from the many other types of dreams experienced during my lifetime— extraordinarily different. During and after these particular three encounters with Jesus, a unique and profound sense of peace was experienced, a spiritual peacefulness that defies adequate description. "The peace that passes understanding" or "the peace of heaven" as described in the Bible must be references to this pure and Holy experience. This sensation was so unique that it cannot be adequately expressed through language.

The feeling of unfettered peace was so deep and so complete that it manifested itself in my physical body. I could feel it swell within my soul as it permeated from the inside out. It was wonderful! My soul wanted nothing more than to be able to keep the sensation with me, not just to remember it, but to continue to feel it and never let it depart. In the midst of that profound experience, my world was perfectly complete. But that heavenly peace could not be contained or restrained. Even so, the physical response to that sacred contentment was so intense, so all encompassing, that it took *three full days* to dissipate. Little by little, hour by hour, it slowly slipped away. Like a beautiful perfume, the fragrance grew fainter and fainter... until it was no longer perceived. The indescribable peace did not cease to exist as it radiated out from me but, rather, was gradually returning to the place of its divine origin. The remaining memory could never do justice to the absolutely satisfying feeling of that heavenly, ultimate tranquility.

The knowledge of experiencing perfect peace was one of the most profound aspects of being in the presence of Jesus. Although unable to continue to feel it physically, the memory of the depth of the sensation has always remained strong.

Jesus spoke directly to me in all three dreams. We were alone as he stood near a large tree in a beautiful, natural setting. We were fairly close to each other, separated only by a shallow, clear stream just a few feet wide. As he spoke, I sat silent and motionless at the base of a large rock in absolute awe of Jesus standing serenely before me. With eyes fixed upon him, my soul listened intently to every single word he uttered. Upon waking, there was the realization of having been with him and the overwhelming sensation of peacefulness.

Incredibly, not a single word Jesus had spoken to me was available to my conscious mind. Realizing the tremendous importance of his wisdom and words, my mind strained to recall them. My intellect failed to understand how it was possible to not remember what he said! Surely, those precious words must be available if I tried hard enough! But only that remarkably pristine peace remained.

How could I fail to recall what Jesus said to me?

Being unable to remember any of his words greatly bothered me for a long time—for years. After all, what was the point of those profound experiences if the messages remained hidden? Over time, it became less important to remember on a conscious level. There was no doubt that my *soul* had listened, had completely understood, and had remembered. The messages had been received on a level that was intended, and that level was a purely spiritual one.

It is significant to mention that as I approached the completion of this manuscript, the reason why the wonderful words of Jesus were hidden from my intellect was revealed to me. On one hand, being in the presence of Jesus took me far beyond faith alone, transforming faith into absolute knowledge that we are foremost, eternal, spiritual beings. On the other hand, the sharing of spiritual insights from those profound encounters still required an act of faith on my part. With the inability to quote Jesus word for word, the writing of this book required trust in the intent of the experience and in my souls ability to express it. Documenting this philosophy was an act of faith itself, an act that also resulted in continued personal spiritual growth. In fact, without the willingness to proceed, the reason for these extraordinary encounters may never have been fully realized. Not only would my soul have missed the bigger blessing as a result of taking that next step in faith, but also, there would have been nothing to share with other people.

During the same time period as the encounters, I spontaneously began to view Jesus in a new way, a way that altered his traditional relationship with all people, perceiving Jesus and humanity in a slightly different spiritual light. These perceptions excited me because they seemed to answer many rarely addressed questions. Eagerly, I began discussing these thoughts with a Christian friend of mine who, with eyebrows raised, cut me off and said, "That's blasphemy!" That immediate response was so shocking to me that I did not mention another word about the subject to anyone for about ten years. There is no desire in my heart to be responsible for leading anyone away from God! Although no longer Catholic as raised, my experiences had transformed me into a disciple who fully accepted the teachings of Jesus. I still do.

Even with the passage of time, the desire to discuss these ideas would not go away. The concepts continued to develop. Again, my soul felt compelled to share them. Cautiously, these views were introduced to individuals with different backgrounds. Their responses were amazingly open-minded, and people were very interested in exploring diverse theologies. Sharing what was in my heart seemed to be helpful, regardless of individual background or religious experience. In most cases, people were not only willing to discuss these concepts, but they also exhibited a genuine spiritual hunger for more. A close friend with a Jewish background was surprised by the realization that my perspective provided so much common spiritual ground that the only thing separating us was religious tradition alone. This same friend encouraged me to write about the subject. My only hesitation was not being a scholar or professional clergy, to which my friend replied, "Neither was Jesus," and that response turned the tide on my decision to share this philosophy.

This basic spiritual perspective works very well in everyday life and offers guidance to live by spiritual design. My soul feels called to this writing and continually seeks divine guidance to please God by following His wonderful Will. I do not profess to be a prophet and desire only to share insight that is divinely inspired through my extraordinary interaction with Jesus. These convictions were not reached through books or other external sources. Certainly, these views were never taught to me within the confines of my religious indoctrination. They have come from the inside out, and not the other way around.

It seems to me that these basic spiritual principles contain a very positive message, one that could act as a unifying force in our religiously separatist world. It explores our relationship with God, with each other, and with Jesus in a non-traditional way. Furthermore, it reveals the spiritual connection of every child of God regardless of doctrine, culture, tradition, or affiliation.

If sharing these views holds potential for bringing people closer to God, a step closer to each other, or even help them consider their relationship with God, it can only be positive. *The Spiritual Philosophy of The Prodigal Soul* seeks to make spiritual sense out of worldly environments and experiences.

Just as an angel smilingly extends a hand to help us, we must extend our own to help each other along the passage home. Some may find the principles overstated, or even elementary. If you find it so, Bravo! For then, you have understood the tremendous power and the consequences of the use of your Free Will.

No one knows the mind of God, comprehends the full scope of creation, or even completely understands this physical existence. At best, we can only glimpse tiny, unconnected pieces of a gigantic puzzle far beyond our earthly grasp. Even so, as the children of God, it is our nature to try. In this light, *The Spiritual Philosophy of The Prodigal Soul* is offered.

Chapter One

NATURAL DISCERNMENT: FEELING TRUTH

Spiritually speaking, it is only religious practices that can be taught. People can learn church doctrine, religious traditions and rituals, and can memorize scriptures and prayers. But the act of achieving true spirituality has to be felt; it must be revealed and experienced.

Consider trying to explain the experience of falling in love to people who have never felt it. Chances are, some measure of love is experienced through family. Thinking they must certainly know what love is, many conclude that love is love, period. Intellectually, it is easy to understand what it would be like to want to share life with another person. But the scope and depth of the difference in feeling cannot be fully comprehended until they themselves have fallen in love for the first time. Then, they would discover a unique love, deeper and fuller than they had known before—a love beyond confinement or denial—a love outside of intellectual explanation. This unique emotion must be experienced first hand and cannot otherwise be conveyed beyond the fact that it does exist.

> **Spirituality must be revealed through experience.**

The ability to achieve a spiritual existence, to actually feel it and live it, is something we are born with. Existing within a spiritual environment is the deepest desire of the soul. The soul yearns for the conscious rediscovery of the spiritual self, aware that it is as natural as opening our eyes when we wake up. Because God is so very loving, we get as many chances to discover our genuine nature as the sun gets to rise.

Realizing there is a difference between what can be taught and what must be experienced is important to understanding the Bible. The principals in the Bible are based upon interpretations of ancient words translated from age-old languages and are directed toward an intended audience. English versions are written using modern language and are based upon what the translators' understanding was, as well as what they believed at the time to be correct. These interpretations, designed to be understood by the masses, have been taken for fact without consideration of other possible significance.

Here is a specific example of how easily interpretations can skew the intent of spiritual messages. Most people are familiar with the saying, "It is easier for a camel to go through the eye of a needle than for a rich man to enter the kingdom of heaven." Taken the way this saying is usually presented, it seems to indicate that it is an absolute impossibility for a rich person to attain heaven. It appears to be an obvious interpretation since a camel would never be able to fit physically through the eye of a needle. But is the exclusion of the rich from heaven the spiritual intent of the message?

In 1897, an American visitor to Jerusalem documented many of the events of the day in a long, handwritten letter. I personally uncovered, authenticated, and transcribed this unique, first-hand account. This letter, while describing the walls and gates around the city, told of how the huge gates were closed at night to protect against robbers. It went on to explain what happens when one of these gates was approached by a late arriving caravan, and contained the following passage:

If a caravan of camels is belated ... what is to be done? There is a small hand gate in the great iron studded door ... The camels one by one are made to kneel. The man walks through and pulls the camel's head through, he lifts or crams the camel's knees over the sill, and then with forcible persuasion if necessary, the camel bends and wriggles through, stripped of all its load. This little gate is called the 'eye of the needle' and to the practical eye of an Easterner he sees a similarity between the pointed arch of the gate and the head of a farm laborers wooden needle used for sacking. So our Saviour, who had – doubtless – often watched the operation, and who gathered his wonderful parables from every day life said 'It is easier for a camel to go through the eye of a needle than for a rich man to enter the kingdom of heaven.'

A camel *can* go through the eye of a needle! This reexamination of the text changes the meaning of the teaching from a seemingly absolute impossibility to an illustration that the attainment of heaven takes effort. It shows that reaching heaven is not easy but, with persistence, can be accomplished.

A camel can go through the eye of a needle!

The exclusionary interpretation keeps people from God while the actual meaning excludes no one, but illustrates that the state of heaven can be reached with sufficient effort. There is great danger in allowing other people to make spiritual decisions for you as they can lead to separation from God.

The Barnacle Encrusted Ship of Truth

Spiritual truth, as often expressed in this world, can be compared to a vessel that has sunk to the bottom of the sea. Religious doctrines, practices and interpretations are like colonies of barnacles attached to the original vessel, covering it with ever expanding growth. Over time, the vessel of spiritual truth has become so thick with layer upon layer of these barnacles that its original form has been completely covered and distorted. Even the barnacles themselves, grown from many different varieties, do not agree upon the truth to which they have attached themselves. So complete is the earthly covering that from the outside it is impossible to see anything but the barnacles without "digging" for the original truth. That is why it is so vitally important to strive to uncover spiritual intent rather than rely solely upon the interpretations of others.

Despite what the world would have us believe, we all already know somewhere inside of us what is true. All truth is spiritual truth. Instead of continuing to react from what has been learned from the various religious teachings of the world, consider other relevant possibilities by discerning spiritual messages through your own soul. This should always be undertaken while praying for divine guidance for the fulfillment of the wonderful Will of God.

The difference between right and wrong normally does not have to be taught. Yes, it needs to be nurtured and directed in children and adults alike, but a basic understanding of the two opposite extremes already exists in everyone. Each soul is born with that knowledge as a direct result of being a child of God. As His actual offspring, we are capable of being like Him, and we inherently know the difference between what is "of God" and what is not. I am not talking about an innate knowledge of human laws or customs, but rather the basic understanding of what is honest and just, naturally being able to distinguish between good and bad.

When each of us contemplates a decision, we naturally know the difference between what we *want* to do and what we *should* do. There is no doubt that the incessant bombardment of negativity in this world has escalated to a point where this natural discernment has, in many cases, been pushed far back into the unconscious mind. However, if you look for it, the fundamental ability to recognize what is "of God" is always there. The moment we consider our soul in connection with decision-making, the choices become very clear. Your soul is always able to discern spiritual integrity and provide clear direction. To test this theory for yourself, approach the next decision you make, small or large, from a spiritual perspective. To help accomplish this, simply ask, "What would God, being loving, forgiving and merciful, want me to do?" You will know the answer almost immediately.

> Choices become very clear
> when your eternal soul
> is considered.

Many people have completely forgotten to give consideration to the soul during the daily, basic decision-making process. If all people considered the spiritual aspect while making decisions, many of the problems of the world would immediately cease to exist.

The more often spiritual discernment is exercised, the easier it is to remember to do on a regular basis. Without this discernment, we continually battle between what we feel and what we think, trying to find balance between intellect and emotion. For every time we have been told to "follow your heart," we have also been told that only fools follow their hearts without intellectual rationalization. When you listen to the voice of your soul, you will come to trust that your feelings about truth are usually right. This is because, deep inside, you already know the answer.

> Your feelings about truth are usually right.

The more spiritually conscious one becomes, the more automatic it will be to view everything in a spiritual light. Seeing things from a spiritual perspective becomes instinctive, since it is the root of our true nature as God's children. But we have to do more than simply uncover the loving nature of the soul. There is a big difference between knowing what is spiritually appropriate and actually doing what is spiritually appropriate. Once we start thinking and acting spiritually, we will begin to be spiritual people.

Over time, it will become obvious that decisions that come from the soul are the only decisions that make life fulfilling, both day to day and eternally. Since these decisions are not based upon the material world, they cannot be altered by someone else or be taken away.

> Once we start thinking spiritually, we will begin to be spiritual people.

Chapter Two

THE CHILDREN OF GOD

There has always been a difference between the image we see in the mirror and our inner perception of ourselves. We are, regardless of physical age, like infants on the verge of discovering our true spiritual identity. While we readily observe only the physical, there is a deep, internal awareness of being more than what our mere reflection reveals. While this is true at any age, very young children are a good example of this. Infants come into this world with a personality and with character. Who they become can certainly be influenced by the circumstances of their lives, but they are born with an identity. Souls are already unique individuals when they arrive here as infants and are not merely blank slates.

Think back to when you were a child. Can you remember looking into a mirror and seeing yourself as older? Didn't you always feel more mature and experienced than the world saw and treated you? Can you remember how it felt when people talked down to you or completely ignored or disregarded your opinion? Children identify with the image on the inside, an image of self that transcends age and is more than physical. We laugh when a three or four-year-old child talks about something that happened to them using the phrase, "when I was little" or "when I was still a baby." All children do that because they always see themselves as fully formed and deserving of respect—regardless of physical size or age.

Being young does not distort the image of self. It is the same as we age.

People identify with a self image that transcends age and is more than physical.

When we are young, we are convinced we are indestructible. We actually feel eternal. Later, as we begin to experience illness and injury, we discover that our bodies are not permanent. Even so, most people cannot imagine their own death, somehow thinking that day will never come. We see it happen around us, intellectually aware that bodies grow old and die, but we stop short of imagining ourselves completely ceasing to exist. Even as the body ages, we continue to feel we are the same basic individual on the inside. As our bodies grow older and older, we recognize our own reflection less and less. We do not feel like the older person our eyes tell us we are, sometimes forgetting we can no longer do some of the physical activities we could do previously. The face we see in the mirror looks progressively less like our inner image.

Only the physical body deteriorates and dies, and on a very deep level, we already know that. We know we are eternal, even if only on a subconscious level. Souls never die but like the renewing of nature, experience spiritual evolution.

All souls, consciously aware or not, have a primal desire to seek God. This is because without God our most fundamental nature is being neglected, leaving a void that cannot be filled by anything else. In addition to a deep awareness of our divine origin, all souls have the ultimate ability to find their way back to God. It is just like going back home to a warm, comforting place you know well, a place of peace where hearts desire to dwell. Souls have an internal spiritual compass perpetually pointing the way home. This compass can only provide direction if recognized and followed.

Souls have a primal desire to seek God.

Failure to acknowledge the natural leading of the soul is the reason that people without positive direction never feel fulfilled, even after achieving success as defined by the world. Despite accomplishing financial security or obtaining every material advantage the world has to offer, people eventually find they are still missing an undefined "something." They are often surprised by this, still unaware of what they truly want. The world alone could never provide the fulfillment we deeply desire because our deepest desire is spiritual; it is not physical or material.

The world alone cannot provide the fulfillment we desire because our deepest desire is spiritual.

We tend to see each other in small, unrelated, individual groups because people have been taught to break everything down by culture, color, country, city, individual neighborhood and by economic level. Even when every category matches up, people still see each other as separate and unconnected. This is the perspective when we fail to view others as offspring of the same divine parent and do not see mankind as literally related beyond biology.

Humanity fails to recognize the true spiritual family connection because of a failure to realize who we are as individual souls. When people do not think of themselves as a child of God, they are not likely to recognize it in someone else.

All souls have been spiritually related throughout the ages.

Greed is just one example of what results from the failure to recognize our relationship with each other. Consider the ties and benefits associated with being united as family. Look at a family business for example. There are the typical customers that the business deals with in traditional ways. Prices are set based on supply and demand, and the business seeks to make as much money as possible for the services and products provided. But what happens when family members need some of those same services or products? They look to their own family business with a greater expectation—because it is family. They expect a discount or to receive the product at cost; they expect superior service; they count on larger benefits by virtue of being part of the inner circle of family. And most often, they get those benefits, without wondering if they received the most for their money or if they were treated fairly and honestly. In most family situations, being treated fairly is a given. There are certainly situations where family members mistreat each other without regard to their relationship, but generally, family means something special, something more than relationships outside of the bloodline.

We fail to recognize our kinship when we fail to realize who we are as individual souls.

Consider how much better we would naturally treat each other if we perceived each other as actual family, as spiritual siblings. Yes, we would still disagree and have worldly problems, but an expectation of being treated fairly and honestly would be part of the equation. Just as blood is thicker than water, the soul far outlasts the body.

As the eternal children of God, we have always been spiritually related.

Once people begin to accept themselves as the literal children of God, they will start to view others as a part of that family, as souls with a shared lineage and heritage. Souls see past the exterior of people ... past race, clothes, circumstances, and past religious traditions. Souls instinctively look directly into the eyes of others searching for the real individual inside. The closer we look into each other the more we will discover the many commonalities we share. We are much more alike than different.

As people begin to view each other as members of the same loving family, they begin to treat each other better as a result and begin to move in the same positive direction.

> Souls realize all people
> are part of
> their own family.

All souls are manifestations of God's Love. Love is God's nature.

Chapter Three

THE NATURE OF LOVE

Love itself is the primary nature and character of God. Without God, the single greatest emotion would not exist. Love is touching God; it is what we call the way His goodness and nearness make us feel. God is always a part of love being expressed and is the reason why it feels so indescribably wonderful when shared. It is love's primary connection to God that causes us to desire the heavenly sensation and is the reason we say, "God is love."

Love IS God.

We are fundamentally connected to God through divine love. Everything God creates is inherently good and divine, making each of us also divine, at least originally and potentially. Our souls are created pure, good, trusting, loving, and innocent. Because we are created that way, we are all capable of completing the circle of spiritual evolution and returning to that state of being.

Souls are an exquisite expression of the magnitude of God's love. The desire to share His uncontainable joy was answered by the sheer power of His Will, which resulted in the creation of His divine children. Each soul is so precious, that God has known us individually since the moment of our existence — intimately and eternally. As the offspring of the preeminent Parent, we each have a spiritual name, a Holy name given to us by God. When we return to God's realm, we will hear our spiritual name again, and our hearts will jump for joy at the sound.

> Souls are an exquisite
> expression of the magnitude
> of God's love.

God so loves us that He continually hopes for His children to realize who we are and return to Him because it is what we want to do. Our reunion will not be from obligation, from fear or guilt, or from duty, but solely out of our natural desire to be one with His abundant love.

> We each have a spiritual name,
> a Holy name
> given to us by God.

Returning God's wonderful love must be voluntary, and not forced upon us. The reason for that is basic: Love that is coerced can never be true or pure. To illustrate this critical point, consider how it feels to be in love with someone who does not return your feelings. The more your feelings grow, the more you crave for those emotions to freely flow between the two of you. Now, imagine that you have a magic love potion, and with just a sprinkle—Presto! Suddenly, your loving affections are returned. At first, you would be overjoyed! It would seem as if you have achieved the objective: you wanted your love returned and now it is. But over time, when that love is expressed, you would start to question it. As much as you would like to believe the emotional bond you share is genuine, you would still wonder if it continues to exist only because of the potion. Eventually, it would become an emotional burden because you would still desire love to be returned for its own sake.

Unwilling love is no love at all. God allows us to choose to love Him because anything less could never be enough.

Love that is coerced cannot be true or pure.

God's love for us is so unchanging that He provides many opportunities for hearts to change, until the end of what we define as "time." Like any good parent, He does not want us to be lost or deprived of any good thing. God wants souls to come home willingly, out of a true desire to follow our hearts and freely return to Him.

Spiritual rebirth cannot be attained until we have transcended the world's ability to sway us from our spiritual identity, and remain aware of the divinity of the soul even in unspiritual surroundings. Until we can maintain spiritual integrity regardless of circumstance, we are destined to be physically bound. Our path, primarily either a physical or a spiritual one, is determined by the choices we make.

God's Will for His children is the voluntary return of every precious soul.

Each individual soul ultimately controls, as a consequence of choice, moving toward God or away from God. With each spiritually derived decision, we move a little closer to our divine Parent. Decision by decision, all who follow God move along a path toward Him. All souls who stay on that path, despite the perplexities of the physical world, will be ultimately rewarded with being forever in the realm of God and enveloped in His perfect love.

Every day that we live and every decision that we make provides another opportunity to pursue a spiritual path reuniting us with God.

Chapter Four

THE GIFT OF FREE WILL

God's gift of Free Will to His beloved children has always allowed individual paths to be chosen. Our Father wants us to *desire* to love Him, follow Him, and dwell with Him. We are not God's pets; we are His divine children with wondrous capabilities.

Free Will removed the boundaries of control, thereby allowing souls to be self-directing. This ultimate freedom is the difference between a free flying bird and one forever locked in a cage, rendering its wings useless. We, however, have the ability to influence the nature and quality of our existence.

> Free Will allows souls
> to be self-directing.

The divine blessing of Free Will permits souls to be not only all that we are capable of being, but also whatever we want to be. This unique freedom we have allows us to be more like our Creator, to love fully and unconditionally, simply from our desire to do so. If we did not have Free Will, we could never love God as much as He loves us. Without absolute freedom, God would be the only one who experiences love in its limitless form. Free Will gives us that same ability, and is the only way we can demonstrate the sincerity and purity of the love we return to God.

Without Free Will, we could never love God as much as He loves us.

The great gift of Free Will does many wonderful things:

- ❖ Free Will gives every soul the opportunity to return unconditional love to God.

- ❖ Free Will gives each soul the gift of individuality and uniqueness.

- ❖ Free Will gives every child of God complete freedom and independence.

- ❖ Free Will allows souls to choose from everything in existence, from holiness to corruption.

- ❖ Free Will permits each soul to affect their environment through actions and perspective.

- ❖ Free Will entitles souls to existence with or without the inclusion of God.

- ❖ Free Will makes each soul fully responsible for the quality and nature of existence.

This total freedom we all have is very potent and extremely powerful. How we decide to exercise it not only defines who we are but also who we will become. The power of Free Will can keep us outside of heaven or take us there. Outside of God's love, it is the strongest determining force that exists.

When God gave souls Free Will, it put the responsibility for the state of our being squarely in our own hands and hearts, so much so that it affects both day-to-day living as well as eternity.

The use of Free Will can keep us from reaching heaven or take us there.

God gave us Free Will knowing that His children could choose to make decisions that would result in their being separated from Him. Consider the story of Adam and Eve. Could the **Tree of Knowledge of Good and Evil** be a symbol for Free Will itself? God made it very clear that His Will was avoidance of the tree, but He did not prevent that from happening by controlling Adam and Eve. God, being all-powerful, could certainly have made it impossible to disobey and to access the tree if He wanted to force conformity.

Instead of coercing obedience, God forewarned Adam and Eve because He knew the consequences would be hurtful to His precious children. Contrary to the lies of the serpent, God was not withholding something good, something "of God" from them. In fact, if God's directions were heeded, they would have been able to remain in a realm where everything was "of God." Souls were created Holy, uncontaminated, and pristine, and God did not want them to unwittingly separate themselves from Him and suffer as a result. He advised against eating from the tree because of His deep love for them, desiring to protect innocent souls from being exposed to evil.

When Eve first took the apple, unmasking the evil she did not know existed, she exercised her freedom through Free Will. Adam followed suit, taking the apple regardless of the clear instructions and wishes of God. They opened the door and allowed ungodliness into their otherwise pristine souls. When Adam and Eve decided to eat the apple, they were in effect choosing their own path, a path separate and independent from God. As a result, they became aware of

their freedom and ultimately of the consequences of exercising it apart from the Will of God. Adam and Eve deliberately decided to follow their own will, which resulted in immediate disconnection from God.
Souls do it every day.

God does not force conformity.

Adam and Eve, in effect, removed themselves from intimate unity with God because they acted contrary to His Will knowingly and voluntarily. That is why they tried to hide themselves in the garden. They hid because they already knew what they had done was in direct opposition to God. Realizing they were naked and being ashamed is a symbol of the loss of total innocence and purity available only when in harmony with God.

REDEFINING SIN

Anything that separates souls from God is sin. Sin is the state of existence without God; it is the absence of God. The word "separation" could replace the word "sin," and the meaning remains exactly the same. When souls follow God's Will, sin vanishes. That is why our Father can forgive us over and over again, because forgiveness is granted when we are no longer disconnected because our will follows God's.

How can we consistently follow God's Will? By maintaining spiritual focus, allowing us to consciously make decisions from a spiritual perspective. When our Will coincides with the Will of God, we are one with Him. It is always one way or the other and never both. Souls either give consideration to God or turn their backs to Him.

Anything that disconnects souls from God is sin.

Discernment of truth also applies to the discernment of sin. We know, without having to be taught, what sin is. Souls feel it. The children of God know when actions result in isolation from Him. We know when our decisions please God, and we know when they do not because of the intent behind them.

Consider the simplicity of the Ten Commandments. They identify easily understood, uncomplicated principles such as do not kill, do not lie, do not steal, etc. None of the commandments are difficult to comprehend. It is only when our Will to do them anyway, for whatever reason, gets in the way. Except for extreme examples, when people violate these primary behavioral principles, they are well aware of their actions. Free Will allows violations, but even if they do not believe in God, they know when actions and intentions are wrong. Without God, they believe that there are no consequences unless they are "caught."

Regardless of the level of awareness, the spiritual effects of godlessness include being farther yet from God and being destined to repeat the cycle of negativity. Souls are free to continue this cycle of being distant from God as long as they wish. They created it, and they will keep getting farther and farther away from God unless, and until, they choose to make decisions restoring spiritual direction.

People know when actions detach them from God.

The chaotic, woeful aspects of the world we live in today are a direct result of generation upon generation of people ignoring the spiritual consequences of actions. So consumed by the demands and distractions of the physical world, many people have forgotten the very existence of their eternal soul.

The First Sin

Some religious doctrines teach that we are born with sin inherited from the actions of other souls, that we are specifically guilty of the sins committed by Adam and Eve. The concept is referred to as Original Sin. However, we each individually have separated ourselves from God. Souls are not responsible for the Free Will actions of Adam and Eve; souls are guilty of the same act of separation. Our first sin was the initial incident when each soul behaved contrary to the Will of God, which resulted in distance from Him.

It is very important to understand that this distance from God is not a punishment from God. We create circumstances by virtue of our decisions, so actually, we punish ourselves. When we do not follow God's Will, we leave God's presence. Sin does not exist in the presence of God, it flees from His sight. Wickedness must flee because our perfect Father is so sacred and so Holy that only those acting within His Will can be near Him. We cannot dwell in His presence when we do not follow His loving Will. We have left Him. Our surroundings are a result of the choices we have made in the past, and those we make today. God does not leave us; we leave God.

Sin is not inherited from the acts of other souls.

Let us consider self-initiated separation in another way. Picture a young boy who has left the comfort and security of his first home. This lad thinks he has matured and knows what is best for him, imagining only the possible benefits of being on his own. No longer subject to house rules, he can eat whatever and whenever he wants—he can wear whatever he desires—he is able to stay up all night— he has total freedom and independence. No longer is anyone telling him what to do. Surely, he thinks any price is worth exercising total freedom! When the reality of his new environment is revealed, he may discover he does not have adequate shelter—his clothes have worn out and he is cold—he does not have enough resources and is hungry—and no one is telling him what to do! His days become so consumed with the many details of physical survival that it completely distracts his conscious mind. He thinks of little else.

But in that comforting place, the haven the child left behind, there is still ample clothing, warm shelter, and hot food is served every day. The loving parents have not punished the child for leaving. Instead, they are concerned and wish their wandering offspring would safely return. But only the child can make that happen by focusing once again on that loving environment and deciding to go back home. The child walked away, becoming voluntarily disassociated from his original surroundings. Nothing was ever withheld but was lost solely through the use of Free Will.

And just like that child, we can at any time return to the love and comfort of our first home and have much more than we ever needed. We just have to decide to do so and change from a worldly focus to a spiritual one.

God does not leave souls; souls leave God.

We have all, at some point, isolated ourselves from God. If we had never acted contrary to the Will of God, we would have remained in His Holy presence. All souls who knowingly acted contrary to God's Will fell away from Him. All of us still existing in this physical state are the souls who fell. We are the prodigal souls. Only the fallen have subjected themselves to evil and godlessness in the first place. As a result, we have entered onto a long path of subsequent decisions. Through the tremendous power of our freedom, the option of direction is always ours.

Ego versus Spirit

When people continually exercise Free Will without spiritual regard, they are open to being completely consumed by ego and being solely defined by the physical world. Ego, the expression of the physical self, is forceful and can only be held in check by spiritual awareness. When ego has its way, the soul is not considered. This world, where the memory of our previous spiritual existence is extremely clouded, bombards us with situations forcing us to respond constantly. As souls get farther from God, it becomes more difficult for them to remember their divine origin and the utter importance of their decisions.

It is vital to remember that ego, your physical personality, always tries to speak first. And if ego has control, it will have the last word as well. That is why it can be so difficult to maintain spiritual focus. There is nothing similar about the way the soul and the ego look at decision-making. Ego expresses concern only for the physical, worldly, material here and now, while the soul focuses on God and eternity. Ego can act as a spiritual roadblock, seemingly striving to prevent souls from following a spiritual path over a physical one, because if the spiritual path is recognized and followed, ego cannot survive.

Ego exists only in the physical world and therefore must surrender to the supremacy of the enlightened soul.

There is nothing similar in the way the ego and the soul make decisions.

In order to achieve consistent spiritual focus, it is helpful to develop an automatic mechanism to trigger spiritual consideration. Over time, responding from a spiritual perspective will become the most natural thing to do. Since we are God's children, we need only to awaken spiritual consciousness.

The demanding physical body can be used as a trigger for spiritual thought. One way is to resolve to feed your soul every single time you feed your body. The body does not "forget" to seek nourishment, reminding you without fail when it is hungry. It is a mechanism operating automatically and without thought every single day and can be used to initiate the nurturing of your soul.

Commit your mind to having a conversation with God before eating *anything*. Every single time—all day long— each and every day. I am not talking about only thanking God for creating the food itself, although that is appropriate, too. Just saying "thank you" is enough to begin with, as long as it causes your conscious mind to go to a place that fully acknowledges God. When blessings are recognized and appreciated, it is easy to be thankful. The content or length of what you say, or think, is not as important as the persistent, frequent contact with God. Perpetual contact with God liberates our true spiritual nature.

Regardless of the method used, the important aspect is to find a way to use your conscious mind to habitually and routinely initiate spiritual thought. Over time, spiritual focus comes forward into everyday living, as opposed to being secondary to the immediate responses of the physical self. Once you are able to maintain spiritual focus, you will be able to recognize the godliness in everything and everyone, regardless of circumstances.

> Ego exists only in the physical world
> and must surrender to
> the enlightened soul.

Because our Father loves us so much, every situation we face is really an opportunity to unite once again with Him. People have countless opportunities to approach God. We make hundreds of decisions every day, but there ultimately exists only two outcomes or directions. Every decision of spiritual consequence either moves souls closer to God or farther away from God.

> Regular contact with God
> liberates our
> true spiritual nature.

Embracing *or* rejecting God's perfect Will is what Free Will is all about. Each individual soul has total freedom, making every journey an extremely personal one.

THE AWESOME POWER OF FREE WILL

The force of Free Will is so powerful that changes or tasks are the most difficult when we really do not embrace them.

Do you recall the saying; "Be careful what you ask for, because you just might get it"? This is very true because we are quite capable of achieving what we desire. That is one reason why people can accomplish amazing things.

Consider two individuals approaching the discontinuation of the same detrimental habit. For this example, the habit is smoking. Aware that the habit is detrimental to health, the first person is encouraged by friends and family to stop smoking. The individual attempts the behavior change because of the desires of others, but it is not what the individual really wants to do. Repeatedly, the cycle of attempting to break the habit continues without success. This person has demonstrated a willingness to make the *attempt* without the genuine desire to make the *change*. The attempt to stop smoking falls short because it is without the use of the power of Free Will.

Changes are the most difficult when we do not embrace them.

The second smoker is an athlete who has come to realize that the effects of smoking are hindering performance. A choice is made between sacrificing lung capacity or discontinuing the smoking habit in order to be the best possible athlete. It becomes a question of what is more important. This individual ultimately decides to be healthy and resolves to quite smoking. This decision, based on a change of heart, is not an attempt to please someone else. And because it was based upon a genuine desire to change, the individual has the indisputable ability to succeed.

Being children of God, we attempt to be creators like our heavenly Parent. Souls have great power to influence the world around us. Sometimes this is positive and sometimes very negative. Regardless of conscious awareness, we use our persistent Free Will to manipulate our surroundings, turning them into what we perceive them to be.

The earth was created perfectly to provide not only all that is required, but far more. Everything we could ever need existed here before we interacted with it. Consider the perfect balance of nature. We cannot improve upon it. Nevertheless, we attempt to recreate what God has made, and since that cannot be improved upon, we destroy instead of create.

Many of the environmental problems we face today, for example, smog and acid rain, are the consequences of interfering with God's natural order. Many flood catastrophes could be avoided if we respected the power of water in nature and stopped trying to exercise absolute control over it. People defiantly continue to build on dry riverbeds, in canyons, and on flood plains. Then, when disaster strikes, people wonder how God can allow whole communities to be washed away, devastating families. Arrogant and egotistical, our modern civilization thinks it can overcome and control many aspects of nature instead of attempting to live in balance with the natural world.

> **Attempts to re-create what God has made result in destruction.**

Humans can achieve living in balance with nature. In fact, it has been achieved. The Native Americans, as well as many aboriginal groups all over the world, are good examples. They existed by reverently utilizing the resources provided by God through nature, without attempting to control or contain them. They knew they did not own the land and recognized the earth as a divine gift. The eyes of these non-materialistic peoples were open to the unique blessings of each season. They followed herds rather than trying to dominate them. Using only the resources they needed, they moved on before the land was damaged by their interaction. Fully dependent upon nature for survival, they did not hunt for sport or waste even the most common natural resources. They remained intimately connected with nature for thousands of years and, as a result of that lifestyle, did not harm ecological balances. Their reverence for the bountiful gifts of nature kept them close to God.

By misinterpreting the ways of indigenous peoples, non-natives considered them to be uncivilized. I find it ironic that when outsiders first saw this simple, natural lifestyle, they called these enlightened souls "savages." They failed to recognize the naturally spiritual lives led by the children of Mother Earth.

Divine Free Will:

- ❖ Free Will gives every soul the opportunity to return unconditional love to God.

- ❖ Free Will gives each soul the gift of individuality and uniqueness.

- ❖ Free Will gives every child of God complete freedom and independence.

- ❖ Free Will allows souls to choose from everything in existence, from holiness to corruption.

- ❖ Free Will permits each soul to affect their environment through actions and perspective.

- ❖ Free Will entitles souls to existence with or without the inclusion of God.

- ❖ Free Will makes each soul fully responsible for the quality and nature of existence.

Chapter Five

God's Will

In the past, I prayed for God's Will to unfold without any understanding of what His Will might actually be. Regardless of what happened, whether viewing situations as positive or negative, my desire was for whatever suited God's seemingly mysterious purposes. That perspective was praying like a sheep offering itself for the slaughter in God's name. Gradually, the realization came that the Will of God is only and always good. God has not created anything negative or evil.

If we try to comprehend the complexities of God, we will never understand the scope because it is beyond our human understanding. True wisdom is realizing how little of the whole picture is seen and how much we do not know.

Jesus told us to come with the faith of a child because children look at things in simple terms. By also seeking simplicity, we can hope to comprehend spiritual intent.

The Will of God is only and always good.

Determining spiritual intent is similar to the difference between the "spirit of the law" and the "letter of the law." Laws were originally made with a spirit of justice with the intention of being equitable and fair. Laws are written to solve problems. However, implementation is another story. Lawyers more often argue in court to win cases rather than for the purpose of determining the truth or what is fair. There is little concern regarding the spirit in which legalities were instituted. It has become so convoluted that the entire legal system has evolved far beyond what it was originally meant to accomplish. Today, there are so many laws because we attempt to implement them word for word. Contracts have become so complicated and wordy because disputes are settled based solely upon the language used, allowing a single word to negate entire agreements.

It is similar with the Bible. After many hundreds of years of translation, the intent and the practice may no longer be the same things. Many spiritual truths have become clouded in ritual. Other teachings are skewed by a particular slant on interpretation and application. That is why it is vitally important to seek spiritual insight and discern spiritual intent for ourselves.

Everything that God teaches us is really a blessing, another heavenly opportunity. If God wished to have complete control over us, He would not have given us Free Will in the first place. Spiritual laws do not exist to control us — they exist to help bring souls back into unity with God.

All of God's Laws are Blessings.

Jesus explained that the Sabbath was made for man, not man for the Sabbath. That changes observing the Sabbath from a rule over us to a spiritual opportunity to commune with God, reminding us to rest from the cares of the world and focus once again upon our spiritual well-being. Observance of the Sabbath is there to help keep us from being completely consumed by the physical world, forgetting that we are foremost the children of God. People can enter a house of worship every week, or even every day, and still fail to keep the Sabbath Holy. Simply walking into a building does not fulfill the spiritual intent; it is contact with God that keeps the Sabbath Holy, regardless of the place. Communication with God should be a daily, continual occurrence, transforming every day into the Sabbath.

Observing the Sabbath reminds us to thank God for the love He pours constantly upon us.

> Daily communication with God
> transforms every day
> into the Sabbath.

Even the Ten Commandments are spiritual blessings and not merely laws. Behavior resulting in being blessed is optional, while laws and rules are imposed by force. However, God does not force souls to comply.

The Ten Commandments spell out the minimum behavioral prerequisites that must be met to be in unity with God. They are only seen as a hardship by those ignoring the health of the soul. Souls connected to God realize these are blessings and naturally desire to follow them, having no will to do otherwise. Souls intimately united with God would not need to know the commandments exist, or even be told they are required to follow them, because responding from love supercedes ill intent. Actions without love are actions without God.

> Responding from love
> always supercedes ill intent.

The Ten Commandments are really directions back to God's Kingdom. They are like a map, but can only lead the souls that resolve to follow them by embracing a loving spiritual perspective. How different might we view them if these principals were called the Ten Spiritual Objectives. Once they are all faithfully fulfilled, the state of heaven is attained! Think of the following as the recipe to feed your soul:

> Directions to God: Simultaneously blend all of the following ingredients into your conscious world. Allow love to rise to the top. Experience the joy, realizing the only burden remaining is to be without God. Proceed to heaven.

THE TEN SPIRITUAL OBJECTIVES

- Love God *first* and *more* than anything else.
- Worship God from *inside* your soul.
- Use God's name *only* when referring to Him.
- Regularly rest from the cares of the world and *focus* on your eternal soul.
- Love *all* of God's Children equally.
- Realize nothing you could steal is *ever* worth the price of your precious soul.
- Revere *all* life, and all of God's creations.
- Be devoted, faithful, and *worthy* of trust.
- Always speak the *truth*.
- Seek *eternal* treasures over temporary ones.

> Hint - When love is first and absolute, the rest of the list always takes care of itself!

All of the lessons God gives us exist for our benefit—to guide us—to keep souls safe from harm—and to reunite the lost with His amazing love. Consider forgiveness, for example. The message imploring us to forgive each other is simple, but many people have a hard time understanding how choosing not to forgive someone is detrimental. After all, they are not to blame! Forgiveness is not a chore or a hardship; it is an opportunity to further the spirit. Forgiveness is a gift for both the forgiver and the forgiven, because it transforms negative feelings into loving ones. Forgiveness allows change toward perception and outlook. If we hold onto resentment and blame, love remains blocked from us. This includes even forgiving ourselves. Holding onto detrimental attitudes and emotions is harmful to every single aspect of health, including mental, physical, and spiritual well-being.

Refusing to forgive is like standing in the rain under an umbrella while you are dying of thirst, still insisting that the umbrella is protecting you! It is self-defeating.

Forgiveness transforms negative feelings into loving ones.

Souls that refuse to forgive cannot be forgiven. It is really the same message as "you get what you give" or "what goes around comes around, "only in reverse. In this case, you do not get what you do not give. If you do not love, you will not have adequate love; if you do not tell the truth, you will not receive honesty; if you steal, you will become a victim. If you look for negativity, you will surely find it. Because this world offers all extremes, you can always find what you focus upon, making the saying, "Seek, and ye shall find," quite literal.

Circumstances have power over us only because we allow them to. We get to choose—we get to be whatever we want to be and whatever we think we are. Over the course of time, you will discover that as you think, so you will become.

GOD'S PLAN FOR US

When things happen to people that cannot otherwise be explained or spiritually understood, I have often heard the remark, "It must be part of God's plan." Many people believe that God is always in control and that our lives and circumstances are pre-ordained. One of the reasons for this belief is the "proof" that the names of the faithful are already written in heaven's Book of Life. However, this viewpoint relieves individuals of spiritual responsibility. If God has total control, how then does Free Will matter at all? What role does Free Will play if everything is already decided? If all were pre-ordained, why would a single soul be far from God? God would not choose alienation for His precious children. The very existence of Free Will means that we control being near God *or* far from Him. God gave us the freedom to be whatever we want to be. Our eternal rewards and consequences are a direct result of our spiritual state and of decisions made out of that freedom.

So, if God is not controlling us, what then about the names written in the Book of Life? The answer is, God already knows. God is all-knowing and all-seeing. The names in The Book of Life are there because He has always known what each soul will embrace. He sees into the heart of each unique child. However, knowing the outcome is not the same as controlling the outcome. But even though God does not control us, He certainly does have a wonderful plan. That plan is that souls be given every opportunity to return to Him. These opportunities are abundant.

God's plan is that we have every opportunity to return to Him.

The Kingdom of God is like a large, secure boat upon a raging sea. God is the captain, commanding the vessel itself. Souls on earth are like those who jumped out of the boat, thrashing and gasping—trying to stay afloat. God constantly provides lifelines for us to save ourselves, but it is we who must grab hold. Help is all around us, but can only assist if we accept it. We must decide to be rescued.

TRIALS AND TRIBULATIONS

Many people speak of the trials and tribulations of this life as being a part of a giant test. Difficulties are perceived as a test of faith, imparting lessons from life and always leaving something to be learned. When similar situations continue to present themselves, many believe it is because they have not understood or "passed the test." This viewpoint will continue until people realize what is missing. The missing aspect is usually spiritual focus, even though it is the most critical component to happiness and fulfillment. The theory of being tested only holds true if it tests perspective. It is not an arbitrary thing. We respond either from a worldly point of view or from a spiritual one. These "tests of life" actually reveal if souls are moving toward God, or away from God.

The first reaction to problems or situations is commonly from a worldly point of view. The challenge is to resist acting from the immediate reaction of our physical self and to purposely and consciously allow spiritual consideration. Your soul cannot respond if you do not take time to consider the spiritual viewpoint.

All dilemmas construed as tests examine spiritual perspective.

When situations are considered solely from a physical position, the soul inside the body has no opportunity to influence decisions. Perspective is the doorway to consciously choosing between good and evil. The point of view, either physical or spiritual, dictates the range of possible responses. When the spiritual perspective is considered, the possible responses grow in proportion with the wisdom of each soul. Perspective is revealed through response.

> Perspective is the doorway to consciously choosing between good and evil.

Many people use the common saying, "All things happen for a reason." I once believed that myself, because it helped me to remain sane in a crazy world. It was actually an attempt to make sense of chaos. It would be more fitting to say, "For reasons, things happen." Our behavior is the primary reason for the state of our lives. Our thoughts and actions are solely responsible for who we are and who we become. But our actions are not the sole reason for every circumstance.

THE HARD PART

The only truly arbitrary factors in our lives are the result of living within a chaotic world where individual use of Free Will runs amuck. We each have control only over our own thoughts, intentions, decisions, perceptions, and actions.

Consequently, other people can, and do, bring unwanted experiences into our lives. While the saying, "You reap what you sow," is very true, what you are exposed to is not determined by what is deserved. Negative circumstances are not a result of God's Will.

God is the author of exclusively good things.

The choices other souls make have no power to change your direction in an eternal or spiritual sense, unless you allow them to. However, the actions of other people certainly do wreak havoc on earthly lives. In other words, even when someone is following a path determined by consistent spiritual consideration, unpleasant things still occur. For example, a person can be close to God, have a great life, be happy, feel fulfilled and be very well spiritually rewarded. That same person could be crippled by a drunk driver, become ill, or lose family members. But that would not mean it was deserved—it would not mean it was a punishment from God—it would not indicate spiritual failure in any way. Some people would question, "How could God let that happen?" But, God is not to blame. God does not direct or sanction evil and never causes souls to use their Free Will in corrupt ways. Good or bad, God does not control the use of Free Will. How free could souls possibly be if He did?

God is not to blame!

Our loving Father knows that the souls of his children continue regardless of what transpires in the physical world. Because the soul is eternal, God has not, even under the worse physical conditions, abandoned His child. The soul continues, uninterrupted. The spiritual journey is not hindered at all, and the path to God is not blocked, or even altered. The soul is still a child of God, and the path endures as long as it is followed. The important questions are: How did that person respond to and handle what happened? Did that person completely lose spiritual perspective? Did that soul retain spiritual integrity regardless of material circumstances?

The spiritual path always endures.

When you love God and seek to please Him moment to moment, you will automatically do God's Will. To please Him is but to love.

And therein lies the mystery of life and the ultimate test. Can you remain the spiritual child of God you have always been, regardless of physical circumstances? When the answer to that question is YES — when situations and surroundings no longer change your spiritual outlook — then you exist in the perpetual heaven all around you.

True Enlightenment is reached when nothing can change spiritual outlook.

Chapter Six

DIVINE INTERVENTION

Although the use of Free Will determines the quality and nature of individual existence, God can and certainly does intervene on behalf of His highly valued children. Because of His overflowing, ever-consistent love, reconciliatory interventions are ongoing, divine blessings that take many forms. God is always helping us. Many souls require divine help because disconnection of the soul has continued for so long, it is often no longer a matter of conscious inclination. Living a primarily physical existence has become the confusing reality of this irreverent environment. If people are not aware of spiritual disconnection, they are powerless to choose anything different.

How difficult is it to imagine a compassionate Creator who loves all souls, a concerned Parent desiring that widely dispersed offspring be given every opportunity to come home again? God intervenes because He wants primarily one thing from us, and that is the return of His boundless, unconditional love.

> **People unaware of spiritual disconnection are powerless to choose anything different.**

With a single thought, God put His Will into being. The unfolding of that profound thought is endlessly fulfilled. God simply IS and has always existed and will always exist. The souls of His children are also eternal.

In spiritual terms, "time" is a concept relative only to the physical world. Compared to eternity, our measurement of the passage of time is so small that it becomes trivial. It is like attempting to compare the size of a single grain of sand to the total quantity of sand in every desert, or weighing a single drop of water against the combined oceans of the world. Eternity swallows up one second just as easily as a billion years. In other words, our scale of time and God's scale of infinity can hardly be the same.

The aspect of time most relative to eternity is the present. While souls live forever, the most important aspect is the behavior exhibited now. The actions of the present dictate the quality of not only tomorrow, but of eternity itself.

> The aspect of time most relative to eternity is the present.

God loves us so deeply that even as the first souls left His presence, a way was already in place making it possible for them to return. God gives each eternal soul more than only one opportunity to change direction. Many refer to that wonderful blessing as reincarnation. It is one of the most spectacular forms of divine intervention.

Here, reincarnation is defined as a recurring spiritual opportunity afforded to all souls distant from God, providing a mechanism by which all may ultimately choose to return to His realm.

> Reincarnation is a recurring spiritual opportunity.

Even with this astonishing mechanism in place, God continues to intervene for the sake of countless precious souls who fail to understand the reason and purpose of this blessing. Imagine the lost children of God on the earth, making the same mistakes repeatedly, totally blind to the ultimate goal of this existence. Most of the fallen souls have drifted so far from God that they have completely forgotten who they really are. They no longer recognize themselves as children of the Creator and, consequently, do not even consider God in their daily lives. These people have come to think that all consequences are of an earthly nature exclusively, and continue to make the same choices in futility. By failing to perceive their divine lineage, they drift along with the changing tides of ego.

> Many have come to think that all consequences are exclusively of an earthly nature.

So many of God's children continue to wander, spiritually lost with no map, no direction, and very little awareness.

PERFECT LOVE

God Himself is so Holy and perfect that He is not subjected to the presence of evil. God does not abide in the absence of love or where sin exists. Remember that sin itself is separation from and the absence of God. Sin flees, powerless from God's sight. Every form of impurity would have to hide its tormented face from the majesty of God Himself, falling helpless at His feet.

Because of His unchanging love for His children, God provided an intercessor on our behalf. Through His enduring mercy, God created the means by which we are not only capable of returning but also of being shown the way back. He accomplished that with an extraordinary example designed to make our divine heritage and the full potential of our souls known to us. This one-of-a-kind example is an untainted child of God; it is the sweet soul of Jesus.

Jesus has always dwelled in unity with God. Unlike some of his spiritual siblings, Jesus does not make choices apart from the Will of God and never fell from heaven as a result. His pure soul is without sin, perpetually connected to God because he has always exercised his freedom in ways that coincide with the wonderful Will of our Father.

In our celestial home with God, Jesus was exposed exclusively to an eternity of flawless love and undefiled peace. Yet, he willingly entered this earthly realm. Who would want to leave the comforting warmth of the glowing hearth only to stand barefoot in the frigid cold? Who would intentionally leave the Holy realm of paradise knowing it would be replaced by an imperfect environment of hate, offense, and chaos? That is what Jesus did, and he did it because it was God's Will for him, and for the restoration of holiness.

When Jesus stepped outside of the environment of perpetual peace and consummate love, it was to interact with this imperfect world for the purpose of revealing the potential of the soul and to reveal the way home. It was his matchless gift of unconditional love to God and to his family of scattered souls. His gift began with an unbroken example of fully accepting God's Will. Jesus made an unprecedented gesture by allowing himself to be subjected to an environment where some souls exist without God. It is unprecedented because Jesus came into this impure environment while still in intimate unity with God, while other souls exist outside of the realm of God as the result of electing their own will over that of God's Will. Jesus was not going his own way; he was continuing to act upon the perfect Will of God.

Jesus demonstrated the highest level of spiritual enlightenment.

In this way, Jesus is set apart from all other children of God. His place of honor is reward for being subjected to godlessness for the sole sake of others, his fallen family of cherished souls. That is how much he loves God. That is how much Jesus loves us!

In a world that includes violence, hate, and conflict, Jesus maintained spiritual integrity and perspective regardless of surroundings, teaching that love, forgiveness, and the Will of God are of the utmost importance. Jesus demonstrated that it is possible to live from a spiritual perspective in every circumstance and in any physical environment. True enlightenment is attained when surroundings and circumstances have no power to influence spiritual perspective. That enlightenment is exactly what Jesus exhibited. He rose above the physical world and did not give in to it. He proved that, as the children of God, we have eternal life. Because we are forever part of God Himself, eternal life is our heritage.

Jesus entered this impure environment while still in intimate unity with God.

We are all the children of God, including the precious soul of Jesus. We are the same kind of divine creation; although Jesus has achieved more than any other soul. His sacrifice, born of love and compassion, was and will forever be unparalleled. No other soul will ever be called upon to do what Jesus did. When Jesus said the only way to God was through him, he meant we would also be required to follow God perpetually, just as he did. There is no other way to accomplish spiritual unity! He constantly referred to God as our Father in heaven and offered himself as a bridge to God. No soul is nearer to God than the soul of Jesus. It is another reason why we must go "through him" to reach God. Souls on a path approaching God will encounter Jesus along the way. Souls would have to go beyond the level of achievement that Jesus has attained to be nearer to God than he is. When we recognize ourselves as God's child, we realize that all souls are God's children, including our wonderful brother Jesus. We just have to accept the knowledge that we, like Jesus, have the potential to be divine and turn our hearts and minds toward God.

Souls approaching God will encounter Jesus.

Our brother Jesus is our most loving friend and comforter, sharing his wisdom and peace and always extending his open hands toward us. He continues to be the only worldly example of spiritual flawlessness. With great compassion, Jesus revealed our divine potential without regard for his own physical suffering.

No other soul will ever be called upon to do what Jesus did.

Jesus selflessly revealed the true desire, nature, and potential of our immortal souls. In this way, he truly is the "Light of the World." When he said, "I am the way, the truth, and the life," he revealed the most direct path toward rescue and unification with God.

❖ "The way" illustrates the way to obtain heaven is by living from a purely spiritual perspective.

❖ "The truth" reveals the truth of our divine identity as God's offspring.

❖ "The life" affirms that the only true life is the extremely precious life of the soul.

Jesus offers himself as a bridge to God.

Without proof that souls have the ability to return, many would remain lost from the presence of God, drifting ever farther away.

THE IMMORTALITY OF THE SOUL

Jesus sometimes spoke in parables and at other times very straightforwardly. We must decide which is symbolic and which is literal, or trust the interpretations from others to decide that for us. Jesus plainly told us, "You must be born again," a saying widely accepted to mean a form of instantaneous spiritual transformation. Those who heard him did not understand. Many people still do not understand. Perhaps Jesus was referring to physical rebirth so that spiritual rebirth might be ultimately accomplished, allowing souls to be physically born repeatedly, until successfully reunited with God. Old Testament prophecy indicated that the promised Messiah would not come before the reappearance of Elijah. When questioned about this, Jesus responded by pointing to John the Baptist and saying, "There he is — let those who have ears hear." His response, indicating that John the Baptist was Elijah, validates the concept of the continuation of souls.

> Reincarnation
> is the spiritual mechanism
> by which souls have
> opportunities to reunite with God.

Jesus did not resist the assaults on his human body so that we would stop being afraid of, and consumed with, thoughts of physical death. He proved to us by his resurrection that the soul, in fact, continues. By allowing his physical body to be killed, he "died for our sins." He allowed himself to be physically killed because he knew it had no detrimental effect on his actual or spiritual self. He showed us that the spirit is far greater than the body and that physically dying is the doorway to spiritual birth. Furthermore, Jesus fully demonstrated the awesome and eternal power of souls acting within the Will of God.

The only true "death" is the demise of a Godly spirit. While the soul itself is eternal, the spirit inside the soul can be alive or dead. Spiritual death is existence that does not include God.

> The only true death
> is the demise
> of the spirit.

Brother Jesus liberated us from our mortal mindsets to free us from continued detachment from God. He gave us tools to facilitate fundamental spiritual change by always responding from his spiritual nature. He showed us that the things of God can never be taken away from us—they can only be voluntarily forfeited.

THE SHROUD OF TURIN

The Shroud of Turin, showing the scientifically inexplicable image left on Jesus' burial cloth, is yet another instance of divine intervention. The cloth is a testament beyond faith, providing material proof that something extraordinary occurred. The shroud graphically displays the physical suffering Jesus endured. It captured his very likeness, allowing us to see it thousands of years after he walked the earth. The Shroud of Turin is the documentation of a supernatural occurrence. At the very least, it proves the existence of power beyond mortal explanation. Even for skeptics, the shroud provides a compelling platform for spiritual discussion and contemplation.

> *Jesus proved that the soul is far greater than the body.*

THE LORD'S PRAYER

When advising us how to pray, Jesus used the image of God as "Father" to give us a way to relate to the indescribable Creator in a loving, concerned, and caring family way. He began by saying, "OUR Father...," clearly identifying himself as our brother. He included all souls and did not set himself apart to be personally worshiped. The Lord's Prayer outlines the elements vital to living a successful spiritual life.

The Lord's Prayer tells us that God abides in a Holy place where even His name is revered, a place that is Holy because God's wonderful Will rules exclusively. It asks for that same Supreme Will to be made manifest on the earth. The prayer goes on to ask God for only what we need today, in effect stating that when we fully trust God, all of our needs are met. After a request for forgiveness of any offenses, the prayer beseeches God to help us to stay focused upon Him. It concludes by testifying to the fact that only the eternal realm of God is worth pursuing and attaining. This prayer to our collective Father is the example Jesus set for us:

Our Father, who art in heaven, hallowed be thy name. Thy kingdom come, thy Will be done on earth as it is in heaven. Give us this day our daily bread and forgive us our trespasses as we forgive those who trespass against us. Lead us not into temptation, but deliver us from evil. For thine is the kingdom and the power and the glory for ever. Amen.

The greatest commandments are to love God with all of our heart, our entire soul, and all of our mind, and to love each other. And if we consistently love and consider God first, there is no need of any further commandments, because unconditional love overcomes any desire to kill, steal, or lie, or to act in any way that would hurt another precious soul.

THE KINGDOM OF HEAVEN

When Jesus said, "The kingdom of heaven is at hand," he was not referring to the end of the world. He meant God's kingdom is always in reach. When something is "at hand," it means it is near and available without delay. It is here and now, all around and within us. The state of heaven is within reach everyday—we have but to recognize and embrace it.

Heaven can be accurately defined as "Nearness to God." Hell is the nature of the environment that results from "Distance from God," and is automatically created wherever God does not abide. Physical environments have no power to preclude souls from being in contact with God. That is why it is possible to experience Godliness regardless of worldly circumstances or environments.

Godliness cannot be taken away — it can only be voluntarily forfeited.

People naturally manifest the values in which they believe. Perception is ninety percent of reality. For example, if you perceive only negativity, negativity is drawn to you. It can even result in physical illness. Thought affects not only attitude but physical health as well. Pessimists are so busy anticipating turmoil that they do not have to wait long to see the next problem appear. So strong is the power of Free Will that the body actually attempts to comply with the commands of thought. If you insist upon being sick, your body will actually begin to develop the very symptoms you are expecting.

Everyone faces illness, injury, trauma and physical deterioration, but it is our attitude that is of the utmost importance. Each situation has a bright and a dark side, a positive and a negative aspect. The final outcome is the result of the aspect we dwell upon, naturally drawing that aspect toward us. When we strive to emphasize the positive, we draw out the good in situations, in other people, and in ourselves as well.

The most significant aspect of health that people have control over is the health of our eternal soul. It makes no sense to be consumed by an attempt to preserve a temporary body over the preservation of a soul that will live forever. This is not to suggest ignoring physical well-being. But if focus is first upon our spiritual health, the inevitable physical limitations will not confine or define us.

Physical environments have no power to preclude souls from being in contact with God.

If you wait to experience heaven when your body dies, you will die and be physically reborn repeatedly. Souls cannot forever dwell in the continual presence of God until they are able to live in a heavenly state wherever they are, without waiting for some future time. We dwell at this moment within the atmosphere of the heaven or hell of our own making.

God's world exists whenever and wherever souls live purely from a loving spiritual perspective. The beauty of nature is an awesome expression of God's love that is all around us perpetually. We can ignore it or appreciate it. Even as chaos runs rampant around the world, the beauty and peace of God expressed through nature are everywhere. Beauty and destruction co-exist, and we each control which aspect to perceive and live within.

Heaven is the state of existing in harmony with God.

Every situation we face is an opportunity to reunite with God by simply responding from a loving perspective. When souls remain spiritually centered, regardless of circumstances, they begin to exist in a Godly state. Heaven is always available, and can be achieved by perpetually seeking and doing the benevolent Will of God. If you can envision heaven, you can claim it and obtain it now, because heaven exists everywhere that God's loving Will is embraced and done.

> We cannot forever dwell in
> the presence of God
> until
> we can dwell with God
> inside of us on earth.

The Ten Spiritual Objectives

- Love God *first* and *more* than anything else.
- Worship God from *inside* your soul.
- Use God's name *only* when referring to Him.
- Regularly rest from the cares of the world and *focus* on your eternal soul.
- Love *all* of God's Children equally.
- Realize nothing you could steal is *ever* worth the price of your precious soul.
- Revere *all* life, and all of God's creations.
- Be devoted, faithful, and *worthy* of trust.
- Always speak the *truth*.
- Seek *eternal* treasures over temporary ones.

Chapter Seven

EVOLUTION OF THE SOUL

The world we live in today is much different from the world our parents experienced. It is often said that kids are smarter, grow up too fast, know "too much" and are less submissive. While this is a generalization, there is much truth in it. Because kids are souls first—just as adults are—they exhibit traits acquired through experience. They, too, have traveled through lifetimes, moving toward or away from God. They are not new at living; they have been here before.

All goodness is the direct result of Godly decisions perpetuating positive spiritual growth. These are actions that move people, regardless of physical age, closer to God. All negative things are the products of souls moving away from God, resulting in spiritual atrophy. This basic principle is mirrored by the way the body works. If a muscle is not exercised or used, it becomes atrophied; it waists away gradually. The same thing happens spiritually.

The less the soul is acknowledged, the less thought it is given in this life. In the absence of careful spiritual consideration, the path becomes darker and darker as souls move farther and farther away from God. All measure of evil is the result of the absence of God, manifested through the actions and intentions of lost souls living a Godless existence.

Unfortunately, some souls intentionally take the dark path. This is evidenced by innumerable shocking acts that defy comprehension, behavior that continues to decline dramatically, resulting in unheard of degradation. None of these acts needs to be specifically named, as they can be found daily in newspapers in every city and in every country. Souls moving progressively away from God become so dark that the manifestation of evil is magnified. Evil has literally been building upon itself for ages. That is why the fallen soul of Lucifer is the ultimate expression of evil. He was first to deny the Will of God and has never diverted from that path. His soul is the farthest away from God.

> The less the soul is acknowledged,
> the more insignificant
> it becomes in this life.

Fortunately, the more the "muscle" of the soul is flexed, the stronger and more predominant it grows. Souls continuing positive development can bring great gifts into the world. Child prodigies are a good example of this. They are called "prodigies" because the level of skill, insight, and talent that they display seems to be a mystery. The concept of living only one lifetime certainly provides no plausible explanation for this. The capabilities prodigies bring are the result of knowledge and experience that has accumulated over lifetimes. Perhaps as a blessing, these souls do not completely forget everything when they come back into this world, allowing them to share remarkable abilities with us. Usually, that "forgetting," which is actually a buried awareness, is part of the reincarnation design because it facilitates spiritual growth. Being unaware of specific details of former life experiences does several things. First of all, it allows souls to be free to start fresh without consciously dwelling on, or being distracted by, whatever may have happened before. It can be detrimental to be incessantly influenced by events or actions that have taken place in the past. If people consciously and persistently have remorse or anxiety over something they have experienced before, it could interfere with the ability to move beyond that event. Spiritual progression requires letting go of the past, as each personification presents different circumstances.

> ## Spiritual progression requires letting go of the past.

For example, if someone was materially wealthy in the last life and remained fully aware of that, the mind may have difficulty accepting a modest lifestyle, thereby missing the spiritual point of the current experience altogether.

We can never fully appreciate what percentage of problems and phobias in people's lives are the result of carrying fragments of prior circumstance into a subsequent life span. Exhibiting irrational fears of things like heights, animals, water, abandonment, etc., without having experienced anything associated with these fears in this lifetime, may be remnants of events from a different time and place. Coming to terms with residual fear or confusion is compounded when only the current life's experiences are taken into consideration. What is not identified is much more difficult to overcome and heal.

Furthermore, "forgetting" allows souls to confront areas necessary for continued spiritual development. If one is striving to move closer to God and understands where the mark was missed, the only way to demonstrate that the soul has overcome the obstacle is to face a similar situation again. Remembering everything from every lifetime would be like being given the answers to a test. Souls have "passed" the test when they respond to situations in this life with the specific intent to please God.

The truly good news is that at any time we can turn toward God. That is repentance. The dictionary defines the word "repent" as "turning from sin." Repentance simply means to change. When we consider the soul in connection with decisions, we change our outlook toward our choices. We cannot turn from sin without viewing decisions in a spiritual light because the fog of the physical world will otherwise prevent that from happening. Focus has to change before actions can change. You must think spiritually before you can act spiritually.

Repentance simply means to change.

It takes only one decision to turn toward God. Spiritual matters are not governed by physical time. As soon as the loving Will of God is fully embraced, souls are immediately reunited. Souls do not have to live the same amount of "time" again in order to catch up spiritually. The atoning or healing is immediately accomplished by the change in spiritual outlook. Why is that the case? Because behavior naturally follows intent. When intentions change, so do actions.

It only takes
ONE decision
to turn toward God.

Do you recall the criminal in the New Testament being crucified next to Jesus? He clearly had not lived a spiritually centered life, but as soon as he recognized the divinity of Jesus, he realized his own true identity and repented. His perspective changed from the physical to the spiritual in an instant. As a result of that change, he was immediately reconnected to God. His personal transformation was the reason Jesus could confidently say to him, "This day ye shall be with me in paradise." Intellect may argue that this instantaneous forgiveness is somehow unfair. In strictly a worldly sense, the victims of that criminal would be absolutely positive that he deserved only punishment. The criminal himself may have believed the same thing. Nevertheless, divine forgiveness and redemption is only seen as unfair when the physical world alone is considered.

It is a wonderful gift to be forgiven as soon as the heart changes and be reunited with our loving Creator. There could never be anything unfair about that! Forgiveness should be celebrated, just as the angels in heaven celebrate the return of each individual soul. This point is critical to spiritual progression; it takes only one decision to be reunited with God's love.

Behavior naturally follows intent.

All souls have the same potential because we are all God's children. We, individually, have the ability to return to our first heavenly home, but we can only do that after we have disassociated ourselves from sin. Remember that sin is any behavior that separates a soul from God. Awareness and intent is the doorway to spiritual unity.

Spiritual thought must precede spiritual action.

Awakening spiritual focus is merely the first step. Now comes the battle between the physical you and the spiritual you; ego versus soul. Ego asserts its command until judicious awareness makes room for the spiritual voice to be heard. Once recognized, you can train yourself to search for that trustworthy voice before you make choices, allowing for the spiritual consideration souls so desperately need. Once spiritual focus can be sustained, souls naturally realize that the only important decisions are those of a Godly nature and, therefore, of eternal consequence.

> Ego asserts its command until awareness makes room for the spiritual voice to be heard.

There is a natural progression to spiritual evolution, most apparent in the early stages of personal spiritual awakening. As the spirit inside of the soul develops, the way to other stages of spiritual understanding are revealed. This is not to say that there is a specific order or formula to follow for progression. This means that there is always more to be spiritually discerned, revealed and learned, and the grace of God takes us there.

STAGES OF SPIRITUAL PROGRESSION

❖ The initial step is the advent of the spiritual awakening itself. It is the opening of the door to awareness.

❖ Awareness sparks the battle between the ego and the soul for control of thought, leading to the ability to initiate spiritual consideration.

❖ Deliberate, consistent spiritual consideration becomes primary over the whims of ego, allowing the ability to live within a spiritual perspective.

- Sustaining spiritual focus results in achieving personal spiritual progress. It seems as if this is the ultimate goal.

- After achieving personal growth, souls realize that helping others or "feeding God's sheep" is even of greater importance. That insight comes from growing in God's love to the extent that it reveals itself in a natural desire to help others. Furthering other souls becomes spiritual food itself as it perpetuates and magnifies love.

- One of the most progressive steps is the ability to experience heaven NOW, actually being able to retain Godliness in this world regardless of circumstances.

- Celibacy is a step in spiritual evolution for certain evolved souls. Celibacy should never be forced, expected, or required. As one draws nearer to God, the more natural it becomes to lose focus on many physical aspects of life. It is a further manifestation of Godliness, a spiritual gift born from a desire to focus exclusively upon God.

THE UNENCUMBERED SOUL

The soul is complete without any need for subsequent classifications, since that is of no importance in the spiritual realm. It is only physical bodies that have gender, race, age, class, or other extraneous identifications.

Consider the impact of gender alone, a primary difference in physical attributes. The fundamental purpose of gender is to accomplish procreation, although many controlling factors have been attached to it over time. Much to the detriment of society, gender has superceded the spiritual aspect. Societies have imposed rigid rules of acceptable behavior, and have branded those outside of the rules as rogues. Men have been taught to hide emotions and display a face of strength at all times. Women have been categorically placed on the other extreme of the scale and are branded as "too emotional." Men are expected to lead even when they are not suited to the purpose, and women are expected to follow even when they are suited to lead. What these gender rules of behavior neglect is the identity of the soul inside the body. That neglect inhibits people from contributing as fully as they are capable, because as souls, they do not have limitations.

Each soul on earth has most probably experienced both genders during the course of living a variety of experiences. People who recognize potential over gender understand that we are more than what is revealed by our physiology. But even the most open-minded are not immune to the prejudices that have long been with us. All intellectual input is tempered by preconceived classifications. Generalizations are extremely difficult to escape. For example, simply knowing the gender of a writer causes potential readers to make judgements about the writer's perspective before a single word is read. Subconsciously, a female reader may prejudge a man's view as too rigid or clinical, or a male reader may think a woman's view will likely be emotionally centered. If the personal and physical attributes of the writer are not known, the reader has an opportunity to be more open to receiving the information without first sub-classifying the work.

**Souls
do not have
limitations.**

Categories dividing people become further distorted when other defining factors are added. After gender distinctions come race and age. If focus is solely upon our physical and material differences, the categorizing and sub-classifying continues incessantly. It is only when we consider ourselves as spiritual beings that we realize physical differences have nothing to do with the soul. The body does not reveal the nature of the spirit within the soul; the actions and intentions of the heart reveal spirit. Looking through the eyes of the soul allows us to focus upon our spiritual symmetry.

> **Physical appearance does not reveal the nature of the soul.**

Although physical differences have most often been used to segregate segments of society and control behavior, these distinctions do have a place in the transition from the material world to a spiritual existence. Even a single characteristic, such as nationality, provides greater diversification to earthly experiences. There is so much physical diversification that there is always another aspect to be experienced, examined, and overcome by the soul.

> **Looking through the eyes of the soul allows focus upon spiritual symmetry.**

Every day, people have choices on how to perceive and respond to the world. Each life, every living soul, has that same choice. The cycle of sculpting our path repeats over and over again until either heaven is attained, or the world as we know it ends. When time as we define it is over, souls will exist at the distance from God that they have placed themselves. The resultant environment will be whatever each soul has created.

> Every day, we choose how to
> perceive and respond to
> the world around us.

At one end of the eternal spectrum will be the souls far distant from God. These are the souls who did not use their freedom and countless opportunities to reunite with God. They exist in anguish because they exist without any trace of love, peace, or compassion; they exist without God. Hell is not a place where errant souls are sent; it is an environment of their own making.

The other end of the spectrum will be the purist of souls, those worthy to be in the sacred presence of God Himself. Even all of eternity is not enough to fully express the joy of being forever enveloped in God's matchless love, perfect peace and incomparable contentment.

Through divine freedom granted by Free Will, each child of God creates the content and quality of eternal existence.

> The journey of the soul results in:
>
> Nearness to God
> or
> Distance from God.

Chapter Eight

Perpetual Creation

Everything in existence as we know it is changing constantly and becoming something different. The only exception is God Himself. God is the only constant, having no need to be more than He already is and has always been.

Nothing God creates is merely adequate. When we look at the marvels of nature, creations are always more than what is required to continue to exist. Everything surpasses the essential elements necessary for procreation and survival alone. Many creatures possess qualities that are aesthetically beautiful, but they go far beyond the need for adequate camouflage. Within a single species, each is so similar that it is easily recognizable, yet every individual is absolutely unique. Take a close look at the blooms in a group of flowers. At first glance, the patterns on the flowers appear to be indistinguishable from each other. But look closer—much closer. You will not be able to find two flowers with the same appearance. Not only do the colors, sizes and shapes vary, the design of each flower is as unique as if painted by hand. Season to season the flowers are produced, yet no two will ever be exactly the same. The flowers are not simply copies of each other. They are renewed season to season. All at once, they are identical and different. This is the unparalleled variety and creativity of God.

God's creations are always simple and complex at the same time.

Consider how all things created by God are simple and complex, fixed and moving, seemingly constant and ever changing at the same time. Stand outside at any point, and it appears that you are firmly standing still on solid earth. Looking up, you can observe the clouds and the sun, or the stars by night, slowly moving across a constant sky. The perception is that only the objects in the sky are moving. In reality, every single element is moving. The entire planet is constantly rotating. As it spins, the earth hurtles through space at tremendous speed. Everything is moving, yet it seems to be both fixed and in motion at the same time.

The "solid" ground we walk on is only a fragment of hardened magma that is actually floating on liquid rock. It is astonishing to experience an earthquake for the first time. As your body begins to perceive movement, it seems unbelievable as the mind tries to grasp the fact that the earth under your feet is rolling like a wave. Gone forever is the perception of a rock solid earth.

As a result of the duality of nature, we do not readily perceive the big picture of perpetual change. One day seems as predictable as the next. The sun rises, clouds bloom and fade, the moon appears with precision timing, and the seasons transform only to repeat again. There is such continuity to the uninterrupted changes that it appears to be unchanging.

> Only God can create
> with such perfection that
> creation never ceases.

Since all creations are from God, they are able to change, which allows them to remain God's perfect creations. Deliberate creation is the difference between exquisite expression versus merely adequate, accidental life.

If creations were made sufficient only for a particular purpose and moment in time, they would have no ability to change. One of the most awesome aspects of nature is its interconnectedness and ability to transform as a whole. Even with limited human understanding, we have discovered worlds—within worlds—within worlds. Regardless of physical size, each world is a universe within itself, complete, yet still part of a larger totality.

Evolution is the constant unfolding of creation.

There should be no argument between creation and evolution because they are both part of the same divine plan. They are inseparable from each other because they are inseparable from God. Both are of God. Evolution is the constant renewing of creation.

Science:
Fact versus Theory

Many times, scientific discoveries are overstated and over applied, which can make it difficult to separate fact from theory. Here is an example. In the fall of 2001, a television series called *The Brain: Our Universe Within*, proudly claimed to have discovered the chemical formula for love. It reported as fact that "love is a drug," and went on to explain that our feelings of love are caused by the release of chemicals in the brain. The program implied that these chemicals are responsible for the existence of love itself. It went into great detail to explain how these chemicals, like adrenaline and dopamine, are produced, stored, and transmitted. At face value, it seems hard to argue with the expanding body of scientific theory. However, the program was unable to explain why the chemicals become activated, except when involving physical attraction where associated chemicals such as pheromones are involved. There was no attempt at a complete explanation, failing to explore the many different forms and types of love. Not once did the program consider that the power of love itself could be responsible for the production and release of the very chemicals observed.

By means of the slant put on the information presented, science has put the cart before the horse. Chemicals are not responsible for the creation of the love experience, but rather, the release of chemicals is a physical reaction to our emotional state. It is not our mental state reacting to an unintentional, unexplained, or spontaneous release of chemicals. Love itself triggers the release. The chemicals are the physical manifestation of the tremendous force of love. God created the miracle of the chemicals, too. They are a miracle because they allow people to integrate spiritual experiences with the physical world.

> Love is a spiritual force
> that becomes
> physically manifested.

Within the broad-based theory of evolution remain many instances of inconsistency. Consider invertebrates, which have lived the longest on planet Earth and encompass nearly eighty percent of all known species. Yet, even with billions of years of successful existence, they have not evolved beyond the ability to flourish. If evolution, as commonly understood, rules life exclusively, why have the long successful invertebrates failed to evolve into something more complex? They have certainly had enough time for that to be accomplished. Invertebrates have evolved, or developed, to a point of balance with the natural world, and that is the role of evolution.

Evolution perpetually allows the natural world to pursue a point of balance.

Scientists assert that human evolution has taken millions upon millions of years to achieve. At the same time, the "accidental" dawning of human appearance was sparked by an unprecedented and almost instantaneous development of a complex brain. Evolutionists seem to be presenting conflicting information. This "miracle brain" suddenly, and by geologic terms very recently, appears without an apparent evolutionary process.

The basic role of evolution has been over applied, resulting in the suggestion that evolution itself is responsible for the very existence of every living thing. Theory has expanded beyond the actual role of the processes observed. When science mixes fact with theory, it becomes very confusing. In reality, the process we call evolution perpetually allows the natural world to pursue a point of balance.

CREATED IN GOD'S IMAGE

We were created in the spiritual image of God because we are His children. God's image does not change. God did not evolve from something else, and neither did we. That is not to say that the human body has not changed at all over long periods of time. The physical attributes and proportions would certainly be capable of modification as the body also seeks symmetry with the natural world. Even so, the characteristics that define us as human, including the capabilities of a complex brain, have remained fundamentally unchanged.

It is, and has always been, Free Will that separates souls from the animal world. Why else, beside a spiritual necessity, would Free Will even need to exist? Intelligence or the instinct to survive does not require Free Will, but the eternal soul does. The very existence of Free Will is the proof of our fundamental spiritual nature. It is what defines us as children of the Creator and allows us to be nearest, of all creations, to Him — because we can choose to be.

Consider the lives of primates. There is no doubt that they are intelligent, can think, are able to problem solve, can love, and have the ability to make decisions that affect the quality of their lives. But they cannot decide to act with evil intent. Animals act from, and within a framework of fundamental nature and instinct. If human beings were once a primate species that evolved to achieve a humanoid brain, why have the existing primates failed also to develop a complex brain and evolve into humanoid beings? Furthermore, if human beings evolved from primates, evidence of primate existence should appear only in the fossil record, and they should not still be walking the earth with us today. Primates follow their own evolutionary lines, and that is why they do walk the earth today.

The missing link between human beings and primates will always be missing, because it does not exist.

Free Will distinguishes souls from the animal world.

If we accept the premise that we are simply evolved primates, it casts doubt upon our divine origin. And if we blindly accept this assumption, the spiritual nature of our souls could remain buried from our consciousness.

EVOLUTION BY CHOICE

Only the children of God can select change. The soul is eternal, but the quality of that existence is determined by the nature of the spirit. The type of spirit that we allow to inhabit our soul can be one that is close to God, far from God, or anywhere in-between. It is all part of the same larger phenomenon of Free Will, distinguishing the children of God from all other creations. By exercising our unique freedom, we manipulate the conditions around us for the better or for the worse.

> Souls create
> individual reality
> through perspective and actions.

We each independently decide to be Godly or ungodly. God's children are the only beings that have that ability to manipulate the present and decide their own future.

Chapter Nine

VIGILANCE AGAINST NEGATIVITY

Viewing my soul as an innocent child, I always attempt to protect it. The more the peace of the soul is protected and nurtured, the more innocent and pure it becomes. This is because, as a part of God, those qualities are inherent to the soul. Over time, not only can the soul return to that state, but the mind will begin to think the same way. When the mind becomes a partner with the soul, negativity and evil are more quickly recognized. Vigilance is absolutely necessary because negativity and Godlessness are all around and can be found in most situations every single day—on radio and television—in movies and books—in news media—and through negative people.

> When the mind becomes a partner with the soul, negativity is more quickly recognized.

There is a fine line between illustrating the inevitable battle between good and evil, and evil being overtly expressed or showcased. While even horror movies require some elements of "good" because the "bad" needs something to violate, there is no redeeming value to the sole purpose of inciting as much fear, anxiety, and terror as possible. The precious soul has nothing to gain by these experiences, and horrifying images should be purposefully avoided. Intentionally disturbing images are damaging to the peace and purity of souls desiring to be in harmony with God. When at all possible, protect your spirit from being exposed to, or coming in contact with, anything that does not nourish your soul.

Evil being expressed solely for its own sake can be recognized based upon an examination of the intent behind what is being produced or shown. Consider the advertisements promoting a newly released movie, for example. Music alone can give intent away, readily revealing the overall slant of the character of the film. Is the music adventurous? Is it suspenseful? Does it sound light, fun, or easy going? Or is the music heavy with dark overtones? Is it discordant or foreboding? Music is often the very first clue. Think about how the music makes you feel. Trust and follow the lead of your soul because the soul can discern what is spiritually healthy from what is not. To insulate my invaluable soul, I go as far as refusing to watch disturbing advertisements and silence the sound as soon as my spirit identifies it as not "of God."

> Protect your spirit
> from coming in contact with
> things that are
> unsettling to your soul.

Many times, negativity and adverse circumstances cannot be avoided. Everyone knows, or encounters, people with a perpetually negative attitude. Some people seem to seek antagonistic encounters. In those cases, it is very easy to be drawn into those situations by responding in kind. When we respond negatively, we are not responding from our soul but are reacting from a defensive attitude of the physical self. We then mirror only what we see before us, reflecting the negativity. It requires considerable conscious effort to resist that immediate reaction, and to maintain spiritual focus.

Consider peacemakers and negotiators. In order for them to be effective, they must not take situations personally and must have the ability to remain emotionally neutral. Maintaining spiritual perspective has the same effect. Remember that your soul has no opportunity to respond if ego has control. You cannot act spiritually until you think spiritually. One of the most detrimental aspects to the soul is failing to recognize negativity. When not recognized, negativity cannot be minimized in this life.

> **Remember, you cannot act spiritually until you think spiritually.**

The effort necessary to maintain a loving outlook is worthwhile. Not only does the effort further souls individually, but a loving response also provides a positive example to the negative influence. Witnessing spiritual conscientiousness in action can alter someone's path for the better. Negative people expect a negative response—and they usually get one. But when they observe, first hand, someone able to rise above ill will or hostility, that ability demonstrates that it is possible to achieve and maintain spiritual perspective and integrity. It can rekindle the sparks of love and hope.

JUDGING SPIRITUAL WORTHINESS

The importance and significance of not judging other souls is immense. You cannot help souls if you are judgmental, because you have then placed yourself above them. Judging creates a contrary atmosphere, adversarial in nature. People who are feeling the burden of judgement become defensive and begin to "fight back," or completely disconnect themselves from continued dialogue.

Judging comes from criticizing differences. It is the direct opposite of emphasizing similarities, which brings people together.

Judgement asserts that being different is never good. It is always the physical self that judges. It is ego attempting to categorize everything, rejecting anything in which it does not see itself. When we do judge, we are not only revealing our own shortcomings, but we then also set ourselves up to be judged, both on a spiritual level and by other people.

You cannot help souls when you judge them.

It is through the exceptional freedom of the divine gift of Free Will that we define ourselves, making each soul distinctive. Every soul is created perfect by God, so each is fully capable of achieving spiritual perfection. Each one of us is on an individual journey and is in a unique position based upon factors such as experience, perspective, and spiritual maturity.

Outside of the Ten Commandments, what is sinful is not categorically the same, except as defined as separation from God. Other behavior that results in spiritual disconnection is unique to each person. Something that is sinful for one person may not be for another, because people allow different things to come between the soul and God. For this example, one individual believes that the color red itself is sinful and refuses to wear it. If that person, while still believing that wearing the color red is a "sin," wears red anyway, that is "sinful." That person would have to detach from a spiritual perspective and override their conviction in order to wear the color red. Souls separate from God by intentionally acting contrary to what they believe is the right thing to do. Conversely, another person considers all colors harmless to the soul. Because this person believes colors to be harmless, colors are harmless. Wearing red would be no different than wearing any other color of the rainbow. This example is meant to illustrate that, outside of the concrete precepts of the Ten Commandments, spiritual intention is everything. Disconnection from God is the very definition of "sinful" behavior.

Judging becomes a factor when the first person projects the belief that wearing red is sinful onto the rest of the world. The point is to let your soul determine what is right for you, without insisting it is also right for everyone else, especially those who do not agree. It is much more important to be concerned with individual actions and intentions, and not to criticize others for having a different belief system or point of view. Stay focused upon your intentions and actions for the health of your soul.

> Outside of the Ten Commandments, what is sinful is not the same except as defined as separation from God.

Souls themselves do not judge because they realize they are not worthy to render judgement, or to "cast stones." Souls are intrinsically aware that the only true judgement is the worthiness to stand in the sacred presence of God. Souls know not to judge because they understand that if they were faultless, they would be with God in perpetual paradise. Judging always comes from a worldly perspective, not from a spiritual one.

FAITH AND FEAR

Where there is faith, there is no fear. Fear is normally a response to a situation with an unknown or potentially dangerous outcome. But as soon as the same situation is viewed in a spiritual light, faith replaces the fear. Why does fear vanish? Because the soul cannot die, and your soul knows it. When you realize you are immortal and have faith in God, there is nothing to fear. You cannot have faith and fear at the same time. One cancels the other out completely.

Here is a personal example. Many years ago while aboard an airplane, a very severe storm was encountered. The plane bounced around and rocked violently from side to side, which was not too disconcerting as long as the craft was not near the ground. As the storm worsened, it became impossible for the pilot to keep the wings horizontal. As we descended to land, the runway on the far side of a river seemed to rush up to meet us. There was concern that a wobbling wing might smash into the water or the ground before the wheels could touch down. And I was not the only one worried about the landing—there was complete silence on that plane. Fearing for my life, a primal survival fear gripped me and a feeling of panic started to rise, threatening to overwhelm me. In an attempt to regain my inner composure, this question was posed in my thoughts, "Okay—what's the worst thing that can happen?" The immediate reply was, "I could die and be with Jesus." The instant my mind thought of Jesus and of my eternal soul, the fear for my physical body was replaced with peace. After saying a prayer placing my soul in God's hands, the feeling of calm grew. I remember wondering how many other people were praying at that same moment.

The plane landed without incident, and fear was forever replaced by the conscious awareness that my soul cannot die. For me, faith has completely replaced fear.

> Where there is faith,
> there is no fear.

When people worry about tomorrow, they have failed to trust God today.

THE JOY OF GIVING

There is no such thing as a wasted act of kindness. Whenever you give freely, the "return" is an immediate blessing. When you give from the heart, you receive love. Love blossoms around every act of kindness, even when it involves something as simple as helping a turtle cross a roadway. Love is more valuable than anything material you could ever receive or provide.

The most valuable gifts are those that are not tangible, because the purest intent behind giving is to share the blessings of the soul: love, truth, forgiveness, faith, hope, mercy, compassion, and peace. Giving is beneficial to everyone, including the provider. When people understand the tremendous personal and spiritual blessings associated with giving, they tend to be on the lookout for such opportunities, realizing that helping others furthers themselves. If there is a spiritual bank, the currency is love. When you bless other souls by acts of kindness, you are depositing love. Love is dispersed and received at the same time. God blesses those who love, and love is the path to spiritual wealth.

> There is no such thing as a wasted act of kindness.

Whenever someone asks you for anything, be concerned with and make decisions based upon what you intend to accomplish. If you hesitate because of concerns about how resources might be utilized by the receiver, you can still help. If money is requested by someone because of hunger, buy them a meal, or take the person to a grocery store. This way you have assured that your gift was received as intended. You will be all the more blessed because you have gone further to fill the actual need, and that demonstrates a greater level of concern.

If you see someone in need who has not asked for help, and you offer it freely, the blessing is even greater because you have sought it out. Sometimes the people needing help the most do not, or cannot, ask for it.

> **The purest intent is giving the things of the soul: such as love, truth, peace, forgiveness, mercy, and hope.**

People are often curious about the motivation behind actions. Outside of professional clergy, spiritual motivation is rarely expected. If you volunteer unexpected assistance it has a tremendous impact on the recipient, especially when it reveals a spiritual motive, as in the following case. Some years ago, there was a man lying on the ground sleeping under a tree. At first, my concern was to make sure the person was physically all right. Approaching just closely enough to see that the individual was not injured, the fact that he was asleep was confirmed. While walking away, the realization came that even though this person had not asked for anything and was totally unaware of my presence, his need for help was obvious. His homelessness was revealed by the very few items scattered around him. Everyone living homeless and without support needs help.

After a brief mental struggle with myself over whether to let him continue to sleep or to wake him and become involved, I bent down near him and said, "Sir, sir, are you okay?" Slowly, the man woke, and then sat up, startled. By the manner in which he looked quickly around him, he seemed to be thinking he was awakened to be told to move along. After assuring him that he did not have to move, the startled look on his face was replaced by confusion. He must have been wondering why he was awakened. He was not accustomed to anyone interacting with him unless he was asking for something, or was being told to leave by authorities. He asked me, "What do you want?" My reply was, "Nothing, except to see if you are alright and if you need anything." The bewildered man was speechless. At first, he was so surprised by my statement that he said he was fine and did not need anything. It was the middle of the day and I was on my way to lunch and offered to bring him a sandwich on my way back. He said that would be great and watched me walk away. My thought was that he did not expect me to return, even though I had assured him that I would be back soon.

The man spotted me walking back from the deli with a lunch bag in my hand. He immediately sat upright and expectantly under the tree — and then he broadly smiled. He thanked me repeatedly for the food, and kept looking at me with eyes full of questions. He was having a hard time figuring me out, and his eyes revealed many questions going through his mind, such as "Who are you? Why are you helping me without being asked?" He said he did not deserve such kindness and then asked me, "Are you in the clergy or something?" I said no. We talked for some time about his personal journey and the importance of having spiritual focus. While sharing my spiritual perspective with him, he continued to struggle in an attempt to define me. In the middle of the conversation he suddenly asked, "Are you an angel?" Without hesitation I replied, "No, I am just sharing the love that God gives freely to me." His face went blank for a moment — and then he put his head into his hands and began to cry. The love offered to him was of vastly more value than the sandwich. His spirit was starving.

As we talked, he kept insisting I *must* be an angel, even while I continued to deny it. We discussed God's wonderful love and unconditional forgiveness, and the level of involvement deepened. This lonely soul kept looking deeply into my eyes, and then slamming his eyes shut as he grabbed his head and sobbed. It gave me the impression that he had not cried for a long, long time. He needed to forgive himself, and to realize that God is still there—even for him.

I never saw this man again but think of him often, remembering the deep need revealed through his eyes. That spiritual hunger was mixed with sincere appreciation for simply caring about him, and for treating him not only with respect as a human being, but as a precious child of God. When we parted, I tried to leave him with words of comfort for his tormented soul. Without expecting that the experience changed his life, my prayer is that it gave him hope and a better way of looking at himself.

BOUNDLESS BLESSINGS

The power of love can never be contained. Love continues to expand to fill every space that welcomes it. God's blessings are also ever expanding. The more we respond from love, the more we are blessed by that very love as it pours into our hearts and souls.

People respond very well to love and the power of maintaining spiritual integrity, even when it is not overt and they are largely unaware of why they respond so well. A spiritually centered person does not have to announce that fact. Godliness reveals itself in peaceful actions, spiritual perspective and a loving attitude. When you begin to view everyone as spiritual beings, you will begin to treat people like family. The result is very similar to the way biological families help each other. Without hesitation or explanation, people who do not even know you will want to do nice things and to be helpful, and will go beyond the norm to do so. They ultimately respond like family because, even without conscious realization, they have recognized the spiritual family connection.

Godliness reveals itself in actions, perspective and attitude.

The principles of *The Spiritual Philosophy of The Prodigal Soul* are easily verifiable. This is not to suggest that implementation itself is easy. It requires a concerted and continual effort to insist that the ego allow room for spiritual thought, especially in a world requiring incessant responsiveness. Ego rules most of the world we live in. Those able to subdue ego to the point of allowing the soul to be in control and blossom are rare. But the spiritual revolution is here, and the number of consciously aware souls is growing.

Attitude and intent—moment to moment—is everything. Perception is ninety percent of reality, so the way you perceive life will dictate the quality of your existence. You are the precious child of God, endowed with great power. Use that tremendous power to respond to every situation from love—from a spiritual point of view. When you faithfully do this, after as little as one week you will see your world transformed. Once you fully embrace love, you will never let it go.

Love expands to fill every space that welcomes it.

Your Personal Invitation

The purpose of *The Spiritual Philosophy of The Prodigal Soul* is to provide guidance and to assist people in answering spiritual questions. Your questions, suggestions and comments are invited.

The following sources will allow you to contact the author, M. L. Stolte, directly.

www.prodigalsoul.com

This web site provides means to email the author. It also provides a sample chapter, and copies of *The Spiritual Philosophy of The Prodigal Soul* may be purchased.

The author may also be contacted by writing to:

M. L. Stolte
C/O SunStone Ventures, Inc.
PO Box 39064
Sarasota, Florida 34238

Order Form

The Spiritual Philosophy of The Prodigal Soul
ISBN: 0-9718033-0-7
$10.00 each

Quantity ____ x 10.00 = $_____

Sales Tax $_____

Shipping $_____

Total $_____

Domestic shipping: add $3.00 for first book and $2.00 for each additional copy ordered.
International orders: add $8 for first book and $2 each additional.

Ship To:

Name: _____

Street: _____

City: _____

State: _____   Country: _____

Mail form and make checks payable to:

M.L. Stolte
PO Box 1175 Osprey, Florida 34229

Ours is a Spiritual Journey ...